EDGE BOOKS

BEHIND THE SCENES WITH THE PROS

BEHIND THE SCENES OF PRO FOOTBALL

BY REBECCA KOEHN

CAPSTONE PRESS
a capstone imprint

Edge Books are published by Capstone Press,
1710 Roe Crest Drive, North Mankato, Minnesota 56003
www.mycapstone.com

Library of Congress Cataloging-in-Publication Data

Names: Koehn, Rebecca, author.

Title: Behind the scenes of pro football / By Rebecca Koehn.

Description: North Mankato, Minnesota : Capstone Press, [2019] | Series: Behind the scenes with the pros | Includes bibliographical references and index. | Audience: Age 8-14. | Audience: Grade 7 to 8.

Identifiers: LCCN 2018037312 (print) | LCCN 2018039005 (ebook) | ISBN 9781543554304 (ebook) | ISBN 9781543554250 (hardcover : alk. paper) | ISBN 9781543559194 (paperback)

Subjects: LCSH: Football--Training--Juvenile literature. | Football players--Health and hygiene--Juvenile literature. | Professional sports contracts--Juvenile literature.

Classification: LCC GV953.5 (ebook) | LCC GV953.5 .K65 2019 (print) | DDC 796.33071--dc23

LC record available at https://lccn.loc.gov/2018037312

Editorial Credits

Bradley Cole, editor; Craig Hinton, designer; Ryan Gale, production specialist

Photo Credits

AP Images: Cliff Owen, 13, Dario Cantatore/Invision for NFLPA, 23, Eric Lars Bakke, 7, Jack Dempsey/Invision for Papa John's, 18–19, James D. Smith, cover; Icon Sportswire: George Walker, 10, Michele Eve Sandberg, 26–27, Scott W. Grau, 17, Tom Walko, 25; Newscom: Jim Dedmon/Icon Sportswire CDA, 21; Rex Features: Albert Pena/CSM/Shutterstock, 9, Dave Allocca/Starpix/Shutterstock, 29, Steve Dalmado/CSM/Shutterstock, 5; Shutterstock Images: Elena Shashkina, 14–15

Design Elements

Shutterstock Images: GraphicDealer

Printed in the United States 6589

TABLE OF

CONTENTS

PEEK BEHIND THE SCENES

National Football League (NFL) quarterback Drew Brees throws passes for the New Orleans Saints. One place you might not expect to see him is in a parking lot. You especially wouldn't expect to see him dragging a metal sled.

Brees runs past parked cars pulling the sled behind him. It isn't a snow sled. This sled is metal with weights on top. He keeps running. Cars pull into parking spaces behind where Brees is training.

During the off-season, NFL players do all sorts of exercises to get ready for the next year. These workouts help build strength and keep them in good condition. Because pros' careers are based on their physical abilities, their everyday lives are much different from the lives of nonathletes. Here's a peek at life in the NFL from behind the scenes.

Drew Brees trains hard outside of games to improve his performance.

FAST FACT

Most NFL players train with plyometrics. Plyometrics uses jumps and short bursts of intense effort. These exercises include jump rope and box jumps. They increase speed and strength.

IN-SEASON TRAINING

Pros train to win. During the season players train to stay strong and healthy. It helps their bodies handle the stress and bumps of games. Players want to keep muscle mass and maintain their weight to protect themselves from injury. Players also work to recover from the games quickly. During the season, players get one day off a week. All other days they are in the weight room, at meetings, watching game film, and practicing.

Weight room work happens two or three times a week. Workout time is scheduled by position. Linebackers and linemen lift at different times than skill position players, such as quarterbacks. Players don't lift the day before a game. Their bodies need to be rested and ready for game day. The day after a game, workouts are easier or skipped altogether. The schedule depends on injury and recovery needs.

FAST FACT

Players spend about 45 to 60 minutes in the weight room each day they work out during the season. This does not include practice time on the field.

Conditioning staff help players in the weight room.

If a player is injured, workouts are adjusted to help with recovery. Any injury from minor to severe requires rehabilitation. Depending on the injury, trainers use stretches to help the player's range of motion. Heat pads help joint pain and increase blood circulation to an area.

OFF-SEASON TRAINING

Workouts and schedules change in the off-season. Players need their bodies to recover from the physical stress of football season. However, they want to stay fit. Some players need to build muscle for the next season.

The NFL has rules about how often and when players can train, practice, and attend camps in the off-season. All workouts and camps in the off-season are **voluntary**.

The off-season is broken into three training phases. Phase one is two weeks long. Workouts can't last longer than four hours per day. During this phase players only work with strength and conditioning coaches on the field.

voluntary—something you choose to do, not something you have to do

Allen Hurns uses mini-camp to learn and improve before the season starts.

Phase two is also two weeks long. It has the same rules as phase one, except all coaches are allowed on the field. They can begin working certain drills with players in phase two.

Phase three lasts four weeks. Workout time is increased to six hours a day. Teams hold mini-camps. A mini-camp is a three-day camp that gives coaches a chance to evaluate players. No one-on-one contact between players is allowed.

Dallas Cowboys running back Ezekiel Elliott does ladder drills to help with his footwork and agility.

FAST FACT

Green Bay Packers tight end Marcedes Lewis does mixed martial arts (MMA) in the off-season with MMA fighter Chuck "The Iceman" Liddell to improve core strength and flexibility.

Throughout the off-season each player trains for his position. Linemen work out differently than kickers. Training is also adjusted if a player is recovering from surgery or injury.

All players work on strength and **agility**. They use traditional exercises such as squats, bench presses, and deadlifts for strength. Exercises such as jump rope and ladder drills are used for agility.

Some players like to mix it up in the off-season and try more interesting workouts. Russell Wilson of the Seattle Seahawks boxes in the off-season. He focuses on mobility. Drew Brees hits tires with sledgehammers to work his core muscles. Pittsburgh Steeler Brandon Cooks is one of many receivers who does Pilates, a form of exercise using body weight, to improve muscle control and quickness.

agility—the ability to move quickly and easily

EATING FOR PERFORMANCE

Players in the NFL choose their food carefully so they will play better on the field. Eating right gives them the energy to push further. Some pros follow stricter diets than others, but most focus on eating what is best for peak performance. That's often clean, protein-heavy foods. Eating clean means avoiding processed foods and **additives**. Most players don't eat fast food or packaged snacks. Protein helps a player's muscles rebuild after hard workouts and long games.

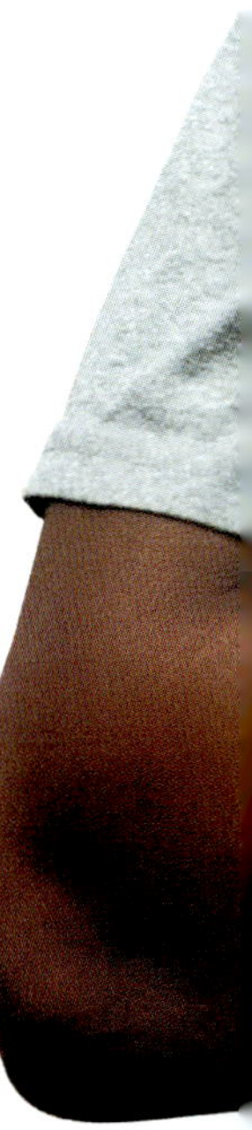

Some players need up to 5,000 **calories** a day to keep their bodies working their best. That's far more than the average adult's 2,000-calorie diet. They need this many calories because of how large they are and how much they work out.

additive—something added to a substance to change it in some way
calorie—a measurement of the amount of energy that food gives you

Players, such as offensive lineman Shawn Lauvao, often have specially prepared meals at the stadium cafeteria to meet their nutritional needs.

FAST FACT

Tom Brady of the New England Patriots sticks to a strict diet. He doesn't eat white sugar or flour. He also avoids dairy, caffeine, and fruit.

Von Miller, a linebacker for the Denver Broncos, eats a clean and simple diet. Protein is the focus for three meals and two snacks. He stays away from candy and other foods with high amounts of sugar. Miller has help sticking to a clean diet. He has a personal chef prepare his food.

Houston Texans defensive end J. J. Watt feels like eating is a job. He eats six times a day. He eats two breakfasts, two lunches, and two dinners. At a height of 6 feet, 5 inches (195 cm) and a weight of 285 pounds (129 kg), his body needs a lot of fuel.

Both players changed their diets once they went pro. They noticed that what they ate affected how they performed. Both Miller and Watt have eggs for breakfast, and their everyday diets are similar. Watt often has oatmeal with his eggs. Miller has turkey bacon, potatoes, and fruit with his eggs. For lunch Watt can eat three chicken breasts. He might also have whole wheat pasta with some dressing and broccoli. Miller follows a similar lunch plan. For dinner Watt sticks to his protein, carbohydrate, and vegetable approach. Carbs help keep his energy levels high and vegetables provide good nutrition.

A healthy breakfast of oatmeal and eggs gets J. J. Watt's day kicked off with protein and carbohydrates.

VON MILLER IS A CHICKEN FARMER

When Von Miller was a freshman at Texas A&M University, he signed up for what he thought would be an easy poultry farming class. His teacher made it interesting, though, and Miller wanted to learn more. This was the first step in Miller majoring in poultry science, or chicken farming.

Now Miller raises about 60 birds in Texas. Miller doesn't eat the chickens, but he loves eating their eggs.

The pregame meal gives players the energy to compete. Teams have coaches who keep track of what players eat. Pregame meals are eaten four hours before kickoff. Half the meal is nutrient-dense carbs such as oatmeal or whole-grain breads. A quarter is lean protein, such as chicken. The rest is fruit and vegetables. If a player needs energy before kickoff he might eat **refined carbs**, such as pretzels. Players eat the same pregame meal every week. Carolina Panther linebacker Luke Kuechly eats pasta, chicken, and lots of fresh fruit.

Players eat very little during games. But they do hydrate with sports drinks on the sidelines. This gives them electrolytes and carbohydrates for energy. At halftime players eat carbs such as energy bars.

Postgame meals are for recovery. Players might have a protein shake or a peanut butter and jelly sandwich. They do this to get protein and carbs into their bodies quickly. Later they eat a full meal.

refined carb—a carbohydrate that has had nutrients such as fiber, vitamins, and minerals taken out

Players have to stay hydrated during games to avoid muscle cramps.

FAST FACT

Sam Bradford of the Arizona Cardinals has a superstition about his diet. He has to eat in sets of three. On game day, that's usually fruit. For example, he might eat three cantaloupes or three bananas.

superstition—a belief that an action can affect the outcome of a future event

Endorsements

Businesses often hire NFL players for advertising. Successful players make a lot of money from **endorsements**. Players don't get hired just because they are in the NFL. They must be good at their job. They can't have any **scandals** in their past. Players can lose endorsement deals if they break laws or NFL rules.

The NFL has rules for player endorsement deals. Players cannot endorse alcohol or tobacco products. The league has its own deal with Nike too. This means a player signed with a Nike competitor, such as Reebok, cannot mention its products when on TV for the league. They have to cover any non-Nike symbols on their gear when they are on the field or at press conferences.

endorsement—a statement or advertisement in support of a product or service
scandal—a dishonest or immoral act that shocks people and disgraces those involved

Former quarterback Peyton Manning does a commercial for Papa John's Pizza as part of his endorsement deal.

FAST FACT
The NFL shows an average of 70 commercials per television broadcast.

Quarterbacks make the most money from endorsements. In 2017 five football players made $8 million or more from advertising. Four were quarterbacks. Russell Wilson of the Seattle Seahawks made $10 million. He had deals with Bose, Microsoft, and others. Carolina Panthers quarterback Cam Newton made $12 million. He had deals with Under Armour, Gatorade, and video game company EA Sports.

However, the best players are always in demand. It doesn't matter what position they play. Linebacker Von Miller made $2 million in endorsements in 2018. He has deals with Adidas, Best Buy, a beef jerky company, and others.

Quarterback Cam Newton has endorsements for several companies, including Beats by Dre.

CONTRACTS

NFL players use agents. An agent represents a player in legal matters with the team. Agents help **negotiate** salary, contract length, and other issues. An agent tries to get the player the best deal.

Many factors determine the **compensation** and length of a contract. Teams consider a player's age, position, and injury history. Some positions get paid more than others. Quarterbacks, wide receivers, and defensive ends make the most money.

When a player's contract ends, he is a free agent. This means he can sign an offer from any team. Restricted free agents are only allowed to accept other offers if their current team doesn't match the best offer.

negotiate—to bargain or discuss something; to come to an agreement
compensation—something such as money given as payment for a service

Former Indianapolis Colts running back Ahmad Bradshaw (left) and his agent Drew Rosenhaus appeared at an event together.

Teams also have to work with a salary cap. The NFL limits how much money teams can spend on player salaries. This way the richest team can't buy all of the best players. The salary cap helps make the game fair for all teams.

FAST FACT

During the 2018 preseason Aaron Rodgers signed a huge contract that made him the highest paid player in NFL history.

FOOTBALL INJURIES

Injuries are common for NFL players. Big injuries can cause a player to miss an entire season or even end his career.

ACL injuries are common but severe. The ACL is a ligament in the knee. An injury to it takes between 6 and 12 months to heal. DeAngelo Hall once missed months because of a torn ACL.

One concussion can cause a player to miss a short amount of time or even end his career if it is severe. If a player has several concussions in his career, the injury can cause memory loss or force him to retire.

FAST FACT

After an ACL surgery, a player will have months of physical therapy to get ready to play again.

Medical staff immediately evaluate players when they get hurt in practice or games.

If a player suffers a concussion, he goes through a concussion protocol. The protocol includes different memory tests that measure a player's memory and response time. Doctors use this test to determine if a player is okay.

Each position in football has different injury risks. Offensive linemen can face injuries in their hands from blocking defenders. These injuries typically take about three weeks to heal.

Quarterbacks often injure their shoulders. These sorts of injuries can take months of recovery. Sam Bradford of the Arizona Cardinals has suffered multiple injuries in his shoulder joints. These injuries have made him miss multiple games during his career.

CHARITY WORK

The NFL gives back to communities. Since 1973 the NFL Foundation, NFL Charities, and NFL Youth Football Fund have donated more than $500 million to charities.

One way the NFL reaches communities is with the PLAY 60 program. All NFL teams take part. They encourage children to be active for 60 minutes a day. Players attend NFL PLAY 60 football clinics with children. Players teach students the value of exercise, health, and nutrition.

FAST FACT

In 2017 Chris Long, a defensive end for the Philadelphia Eagles, gave his entire salary to charity. It was $1.5 million.

The Miami Dolphins partner with other organizations to help give children gifts during the holidays.

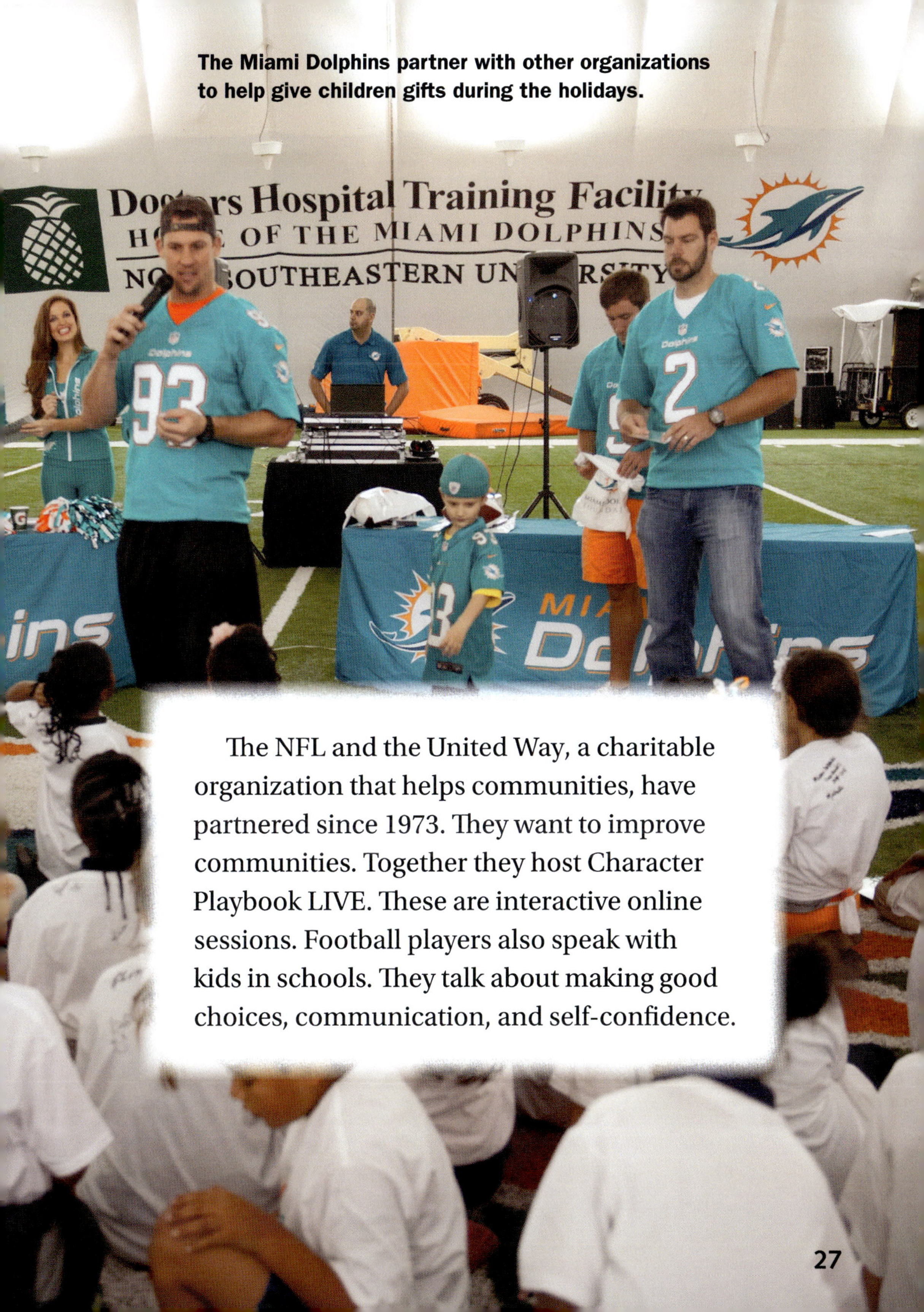

The NFL and the United Way, a charitable organization that helps communities, have partnered since 1973. They want to improve communities. Together they host Character Playbook LIVE. These are interactive online sessions. Football players also speak with kids in schools. They talk about making good choices, communication, and self-confidence.

J. J. WATT: WALTER PAYTON MAN OF THE YEAR 2018

J. J. Watt helped the Houston, Texas, community after Hurricane Harvey. He donated $100,000 and helped raise $37 million for the relief and rebuilding efforts in Houston. For his actions, he was awarded the Walter Payton Man of the Year Award in 2018.

NFL players often start charities of their own. They want to support causes they care about. Pittsburgh Steelers quarterback Ben Roethlisberger uses the Ben Roethlisberger Foundation to support police forces and fire departments. It focuses on K-9 units and service dogs. Former Tampa Bay Buccaneers wide receiver Vincent Jackson's parents were **veterans**. The Jackson in Action Foundation honors them. The foundation supports the financial and emotional needs of military families. Arizona Cardinals wide receiver Larry Fitzgerald started a foundation that helps kids read and supports women who are fighting breast cancer.

veteran—a person who served in the armed forces

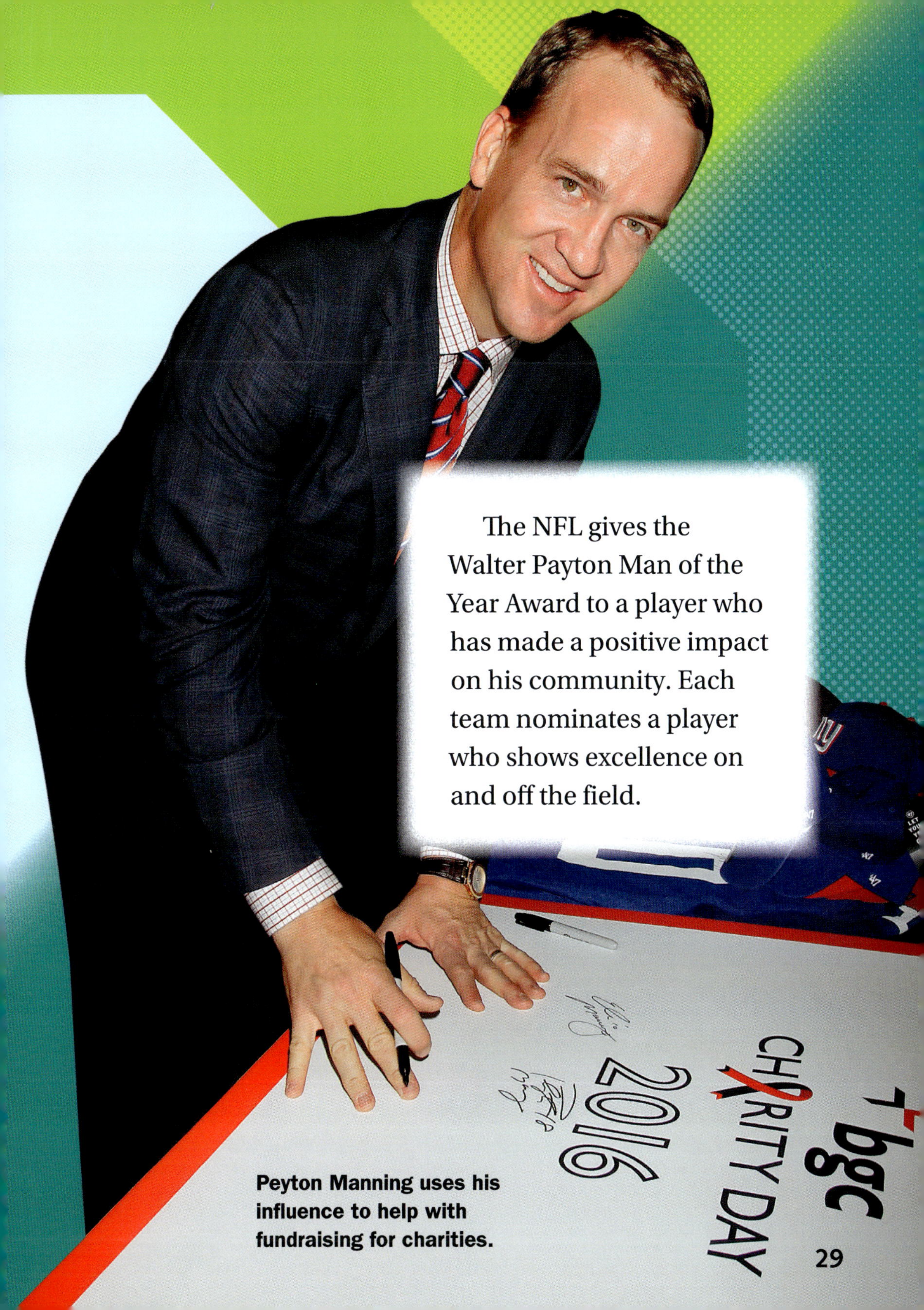

The NFL gives the Walter Payton Man of the Year Award to a player who has made a positive impact on his community. Each team nominates a player who shows excellence on and off the field.

Peyton Manning uses his influence to help with fundraising for charities.

GLOSSARY

additive (AD-uh-tiv)—something added to a substance to change it in some way

agility (uh-GI-luh-tee)—the ability to move quickly and easily

calorie (KA-luh-ree)—a measurement of the amount of energy that food gives you

compensation (kom-puhn-SAY-shun)—something such as money given as payment for a service

endorsement (in-DORS-muhnt)—a statement or advertisement in support of a product or service

negotiate (ni-GOH-shee-ate)—to bargain or discuss something to come to an agreement

refined carb (re-FINED CARB)—a carbohydrate that has had nutrients such as fiber, vitamins, and minerals taken out

scandal (SKAN-duhl)—a dishonest or immoral act that shocks people and disgraces those involved

superstition (soo-pur-STI-shuhn)—a belief that an action can affect the outcome of a future event

veteran (VET-ur-uhn)—a person who served in the armed forces

voluntary (VOL-uhn-ter-ee)—something you choose to do, not something you have to do

READ MORE

Fishman, Jon M. *J.J. Watt*. Amazing Athletes. Minneapolis: Lerner Publications Company, 2015.

Howell, Brian. *12 Reasons to Love Football*. Sports Report. Mankato, Minn.: 12-Story Library, 2018.

Kortemeier, Todd. *Pro Football by the Numbers*. Pro Sports by the Numbers. Mankato, Minn.: Capstone Press, 2016.

Nagelhout, Ryan. *Football: Who Does What?* Sports: What's Your Position? New York: Gareth Stevens Publishing, 2018.

INTERNET SITES

Use FactHound to find Internet sites related to this book.

Visit www.facthound.com

Just type in 9781543554250 and go.

INDEX